RAND NATIONAL DEFENSE RESEARCH INSTIT

T0170233

Implications of the Security Cooperation Office Transition in Afghanistan for Special Operations Forces

An Abbreviated Report of the Study's Primary Findings

Jason H. Campbell, Richard Girven, Ben Connable, Jonah Blank, Raphael S. Cohen, Larry Hanauer, William Young, Linda Robinson, Sean Mann

Prepared for Special Operations Joint Task Force—Afghanistan

For more information on this publication, visit www.rand.org/t/RR1201z1

Library of Congress Cataloging-in-Publication Data is available for this publication.

ISBN: 978-0-8330-9647-0

Support RAND
Make a tax-deductible charitable contribution at
www.rand.org/giving/contribute

www.rand.org

Preface

This report is an abbreviated version of a longer-form report that, for national security reasons, is not available to the general public. This abbreviated report focuses on the long-form report's key findings and implications for Afghanistan. These findings were drawn from examinations of six historical case studies in which the mission of special operations forces (SOF) in country transitioned over time to some level of inclusion in the U.S. embassy's Security Cooperation Office (SCO). The cases of Iraq, Jordan, Pakistan, the Philippines, Uganda, and Yemen are covered, and the interactions and relationships between SOF organizations and personnel and the U.S. country team in each embassy are analyzed. Drawing on existing literature and extensive interviews with mission stakeholders, the report characterizes how U.S. SOF transitions in each of these nations have affected SOF's ability to conduct ongoing missions and derives lessons learned for SOF when transitioning to a SCO in general and for NATO Special Operations Component Command–Afghanistan/Special Operations Joint Task Force–Afghanistan to transition to a SCO in Afghanistan in particular. A full explanation of the methodology applied for case study selection, as well as adopted interview protocols, are provided in the long-form version of this report.

This research was sponsored by the Office of the Secretary of Defense and conducted within the International Security and Defense Policy Center of the RAND National Defense Research Institute, a federally funded research and development center sponsored by the Office of the Secretary of Defense, the Joint Staff, the Unified Combatant Commands, the Navy, the Marine Corps, the defense agencies, and the defense Intelligence Community.

For more information on the RAND International Security and Defense Policy Center, see www.rand.org/nsrd/ndri/centers/isdp or contact the director (contact information is provided on the web page).

Contents

Summary

The U.S. special operations forces (SOF) mission in Afghanistan is scheduled to transition over the next few years. As the nature of the environment evolves to something more closely resembling a "normal" host-nation setting, there will be a transition from a large SOF presence with semiautonomous command and control functions to a much smaller liaison or representational footprint within the U.S. embassy. Planning for transition is already underway and could benefit from identification of issues and challenges faced by SOF, as well as lessons learned by SOF elements and country teams in other parts of the world.

At the request of the sponsor, the RAND National Defense Research Institute therefore examined six historical cases in which the mission of SOF in country transitioned over time from Title 10 missions to some level of inclusion in the U.S. embassy's Security Cooperation Office (SCO). The research sought background and context for SOF missions in Iraq, Jordan, Pakistan, the Philippines, Uganda, and Yemen. The study team explored the interactions and relationships between SOF organizations and personnel in country and the U.S. country team in each embassy, with a view to drawing out lessons for a future SOF transition in Afghanistan.

SOF differ from general-purpose forces in that they typically require unique modes of employment, tactics, techniques, procedures, and equipment. SOF core activities include direct action, special reconnaissance, countering weapons of mass destruction, counterterrorism, unconventional warfare, foreign internal defense, security force assistance, hostage rescue and recovery, counterinsurgency, foreign humanitarian assistance, military information operations, and civil affairs operations. SCOs, by contrast, concern themselves with the execution of the U.S. security assistance program under Title 22 of the U.S. Code. Security assistance programs authorized and appropriated under Title 22 include the International Military Education and Training (IMET) program, the Foreign Military Financing Program (FMF), the Economic Support Fund (ESF), Peacekeeping Operations (PKO), International Narcotics and Law Enforcement (INCLE), and Nonproliferation, Anti-Terrorism, Demining, and Related Programs (NADR). SCOs also manage foreign military sales (FMS), commercial exports or direct commercial sales (DCS), drawdowns, and equipment leasing.[1]

The study team conducted a literature review of doctrine, regulation, policy, and historical knowledge of SOF and SCO operations for each case. We also conducted semistructured interviews with more than 60 individuals who worked in those countries or supported missions there while serving as ambassadors, section heads on a country team, security cooperation officers, members of the intelligence community or other embassy agency, officials based in Washington, or deployed or assigned SOF officers or noncommissioned officers.

This abbreviated version of the long-form report provides a comprehensive synopsis of the key findings of the research and the implications of these for U.S. officials involved in transitional planning in Afghanistan. It is structured to convey lessons learned and, where applicable, challenges related to four distinct entities that the SOF element in Afghanistan will depend on for guidance and coordination during and after transition to Chief of Mission authority. These are (1) other agency elements in country, (2) agency elements stateside, (3) the host nation, and (4) the broader SOF community. Key findings and challenges include the following:

---

[1] Defense Security Cooperation Agency, *Security Assistance Management Manual*, undated, Chapter 2.

Other Agency Elements in Country

Findings

1. Regular coordination with the country team is essential.
2. Clear understanding among the country team of the various authorities that different elements are operating under prevents confusion and discord.
3. Rapport and trust building within the country team can pay great dividends for SOF equities.

Challenge

Space issues and limitations can be a limiting factor in certain instances.

Other Agency Elements Stateside

Findings

1. A lack of precise and compatible strategic guidance to the ambassador and the SOF element can negatively affect planning within the country team.
2. The activities of Washington agencies, such as the Pentagon and State Department, as well as the combatant commands, influence relationships within the country team.

Host Nation

Findings

1. A formal agreement with the host/partner nation specifically outlining rules of engagement and expectations can help avoid misunderstandings and operational difficulties.
2. Building lasting bonds with host/partner-nation security officials can help smooth fluctuations in the bilateral relations between the governments.

Challenge

Shifting from Title 10 to Title 22 authorities can create added strain with host/partner-nation authorities, who may not understand the distinction and may not be content with the changes involved.

Broader SOF Community

Findings

1. Staffing program managers in the SCO who have knowledge of SOF requirements is a good complement to the typical SOF operational liaison assigned to an embassy.
2. SOF personnel assigned to serve in an embassy should be provided appropriate predeployment training.
3. Trade-offs between Title 10 and Title 22 authorities exist: While the former typically experience greater freedom of movement, the latter tend to have better access to embassy facilities, funding, and logistical support.

Challenge

The current cap on deployments for SOF personnel can make it difficult for personnel to mesh well with the rest of the country team.

Abbreviations

CMSE	civil-military support element
JUSMAG	Joint United States Military Advisory Group
MIST	military information support team
NATO	North Atlantic Treaty Organization
NCO	noncommissioned officer
ODRP	Office of the Defense Representative–Pakistan
RSO	regional security officer
SCO	Security Cooperation Office
SOC	Special Operations Command
SOCAFRICA	Special Operations Command Africa
SOF	special operations forces
SOLO	special operations liaison officer
USSOCOM	U.S. Special Operations Command

CHAPTER ONE

Lessons Learned, Challenges, and Implications for Afghanistan

The conclusion of the NATO International Security Assistance Force combat mission at the end of 2014 will change the dynamic of how remaining international forces interact with their Afghan partners. While precise timetables have not been formally determined, current U.S. strategic guidance suggests that the follow-on Resolute Support Mission will last through the end of 2016. Thereafter, all interactions within Afghanistan will be handled bilaterally, and the bulk of any enduring U.S. military presence will fall under Chief of Mission authority. To enable what is foreseen to be a lasting military-to-military engagement, planning is underway for a robust Security Cooperation Office (SCO) to manage the relationship.

U.S. special operations forces (SOF) have been one of the key components of U.S. efforts in Afghanistan since the start of the conflict. Some aspects of their current mission set are likely to persist. Some of these will involve or fall under different offices within the embassy, including the SCO. Thus, successfully interacting with the country team writ large will be crucial to achieving SOF's post–Resolute Support Mission goals and objectives.

SOF differ from general-purpose forces in that they typically require unique modes of employment, tactics, techniques, procedures, and equipment. SOF core activities include direct action, special reconnaissance, countering weapons of mass destruction, counterterrorism, unconventional warfare, foreign internal defense, security force assistance, hostage rescue and recovery, counterinsurgency, foreign humanitarian assistance, military information operations, and civil affairs operations. SCOs, by contrast, concern themselves with the execution of the U.S. security assistance program under Title 22 of the U.S. Code.[1] Security assistance programs authorized and appropriated under Title 22 include the International Military Education and Training (IMET) program, the Foreign Military Financing Program (FMF), the Economic Support Fund (ESF), Peacekeeping Operations (PKO), International Narcotics and Law Enforcement (INCLE), and Nonproliferation, Anti-Terrorism, Demining, and Related Programs (NADR). SCOs also manage foreign military sales (FMS), commercial exports or direct commercial sales (DCS), drawdowns, and equipment leasing.[2]

This document provides a comprehensive synopsis of the principal findings from a longer report that, for national security reasons, is not available to the general public. The purpose of the study is to inform SOF leadership of lessons learned in planning and operating in a transitional environment with in-country intramilitary and interagency partners. The study examines six relevant case studies where SOF currently has, or has recently had, a robust footprint and/or a diverse mission set at the time of transition: Iraq, Jordan, Yemen, Pakistan, Uganda, and the Philippines. The study provides insights on (1) how SOF elements can best integrate with other relevant components of the interagency in a way that best ensures mission success, (2) potential pitfalls to avoid in this environment, and (3) limiting factors commonly confronted, the influence of which may be beyond the control of SOF leaders.

This document is subdivided into four sections, each of which focuses on a partner entity for the SOF component in Afghanistan: (1) agency elements within the country team, (2) agency elements stateside, (3) the host nation, and (4) the broader SOF community.

---

[1] U.S. Code, Title 22, Foreign Relations and Intercourse, as amended through January 16, 2014.

[2] Defense Security Cooperation Agency, *Security Assistance Management Manual*, undated, Chapter 2.

In each chapter, a number of relevant lessons learned are identified and described. These are followed, in most cases, by a description of an ongoing challenge that may or may not be within the purview of the SOF community to address. Finally, each section concludes with a subsection discussing the implications for present-day Afghanistan.

The lessons learned included here are presented in the form of advice grounded in experience, with specific positive and negative examples drawn from the case studies to indicate how that advice historically prevented or solved a problem. The challenges included here are those for which there was no particular solution or best practice offered, but for which the study team provides some recommendation to assist in preparation for or amelioration.

CHAPTER TWO

Working with the Interagency: Country Team

The country team collectively represents those offices and organizations with which SOF personnel will most regularly interact in order to implement U.S. policy. While ably operating in such an environment is, by itself, likely to be insufficient for success, failing to tend to these relationships will almost certainly guarantee that SOF objectives are only partially, if at all, satisfied.

Lessons Learned

Regular coordination meetings with the Chief of Mission and the country team are essential to the success of SCO and SOF missions, provide transparency and situational awareness to all involved, and help prevent unnecessary problems with the host/ partner nation.

Regardless of the operational chain of command, the U.S. ambassador is Chief of Mission and the senior in-country representative of the President and Commander in Chief.[1] Keeping the ambassador and country team fully informed of SOF plans and activities garners additional support and assistance from the embassy, supports SOF doctrinal goals of a whole-of-government approach, and may prevent unforeseen difficulties with the host nation. Whether operating inde-

---

[1] Joint Publication 3-05, *Joint Special Operations*, Washington, D.C.: Office of the Chairman of the Joint Chiefs of Staff, April 18, 2011.

pendently of the SCO or embedded within it, SOF needs to ensure that, where SOF activities are concerned, there are clear channels of communication to the embassy front office and full transparency on SOF authorities, goals, intentions, and missions.

For example, in Pakistan in 2010, an integrated strategy was written to help bring all the embassy components together under a whole-of-government approach. Continuous monitoring, communication, and transparency were required to keep the strategy functioning. The State Department was kept apprised of everything SOF was doing and under what authorities, and Sate Department officials were invited along into the field (with the exception of kinetic operations) to advise and assist under State Department authorities. Additionally, an excellent relationship between the SOF and the Office of the Defense Representative–Pakistan (ODRP) resulted in a portion of the Title 22 Security Assistance budget being sliced off for Special Operations Command (SOC) Forward–Pakistan. SOF in Pakistan kept the country team informed and projected an annual requirement for certain programs. In response, the ODRP ensured that SOF did not run out of money. According to multiple interviewees, if the ODRP had not done this, SOF would not have achieved mission success.[2]

In contrast to Pakistan, a lack of appropriate SOF coordination with the country team in Uganda led to the government of Uganda objecting to SOF bringing in weapons to support the mission to counter the Lord's Resistance Army. Weapons were impounded at the airport of debarkation, and the ambassador's personal intervention was required to "reassure the host government that the U.S. wasn't staging a coup" and to prevent an international incident.[3]

Clear understanding by Chief of Mission, SOF, SCO, senior officials from other government agencies, and other members of the country team of the boundaries and limitations of operational authorities as they relate to mission is critical to the efficient use of

---

[2] Interview with U.S. military official, October 7, 2014.

[3] Interview with U.S. military official, August 28, 2014.

limited resources, avoiding interagency conflicts, and facilitating smooth mission execution.

The issue of authorities came up in every case except Uganda. In many cases, the country team imagined that SOF had authorities it did not, and in some cases, the embassy thought that SOF did not have authorities that it did. In other cases, clear authorities for an intended action or program appeared to be lacking, and interviewees suggested that country team members worked together to find ways to achieve missions in spite of, rather than in concert with, authorities. Most successful were those deployments where SOF worked transparently to ensure that the ambassador understood the range and source of authorities vested in SOF and with the country team and had a clear

> understanding [of] the limits of his or her power. There would be some instances in which the Chief of Mission might have authority on paper, but in reality the actual authority would be some other actor. There should be open lines of communication at the embassy, and the Chief of Mission, senior officials from other relevant government agencies, and commander of U.S. military forces should keep each other informed of their individual perceptions of where the boundaries of their respective authorities lie.[4]

When operating outside of the United States, SOF generally operate in accordance with Title 10 of the U.S. Code, under the command of the Geographic Combatant Command commander, unless otherwise directed by the President or the Secretary of Defense.[5] Alternately, SOF may operate under Chief of Mission authority when performing certain functions under either Title 22 or Title 50,[6] but may also, in certain cases directed by the President or Secretary of Defense, operate

---

[4] Interview with U.S. military official, August 28, 2014.

[5] U.S. Code, Title 10, Armed Forces, Subtitle A, General Military Law, Part I, Organization and General Military Powers, Chapter 6, Combatant Commands, Section 167, Unified Combatant Command for Special Operations Forces, January 3, 2012.

[6] U.S. Code, Title 50, War and National Defense, as amended through January 16, 2014.

under the direct authority of the commander of U.S. Special Operations Command (USSOCOM).

One official noted that "authorities are the issue—they are the single biggest limiting factor."[7] Another interviewee noted that, during the planning process in Iraq, personnel had a difficult time understanding the "nuance and distinctions" between the authorities under the various titles.[8] Others commented on the importance of understanding the difference between an organization chart and reality:

> Everyone involved should understand that the formal organizational chart does not necessarily reflect the de facto chain of command. The Chief of Mission will have ultimate say over SOF operations—except when he or she doesn't.[9]

> There will always be instances in which some SOF personnel are conducting missions at the military chain of command or senior members of other relevant government agencies. It's vital for all players (Chief of Mission, U.S. military commander, senior members of other relevant government agencies) to have a shared understanding of when each of them will be the ultimate shot-caller.[10]

To achieve full integration and optimal success in country, the SOF element should consider ways to build rapport and gain trust with the country team, even if there is no immediate benefit. This means first determining where the most useful bridges should be built (U.S. Agency for International Development, other government agencies, Public Diplomacy Office, etc.).

Relationships in an embassy should not be considered transactional, but part of an overall strategy designed to develop access across the entire country team. Building rapport with all of the embassy's

---

[7] Interview with U.S. military official, September 3, 2014.

[8] Interview with U.S. military official, October 1, 2014.

[9] Interview with U.S. military official, September 7, 2014.

[10] Interview with U.S. military official, September 8, 2014.

"informal powerbrokers," those who clearly have the trust of the ambassador, is an important aspect of working in a SCO or within the embassy environment.[11] As one official noted, "as a military element in an embassy, you constantly have to prove that you are a value add to the U.S. embassy. One week you can be the golden child, but the next week you have to re-prove your utility."[12]

Officials noted that too often SOF view embassy billets or positions as "plug and play," which is detrimental. "You can't just pluck a guy of a predetermined rank and place them in a billet, especially not in an embassy," according to one interviewee.[13] Integration of SOF authorities in an embassy environment requires an attitude that supports an ongoing relationship and an understanding that the country team is working toward long-term goals. Finding ways to assist other elements of the embassy in achieving their goals can go a long way toward building improved access, even if some short-term SOF goals need to be put hold. As one SOF officer suggested, "SOF guys need to understand that some broader strategic considerations go into embassy decisions, and they should not get overly focused on implementing or completing smaller, tactical issues."[14]

Appointing personnel with experience working in an embassy environment can be beneficial for all parties. Several officers interviewed suggested that having SOF-experienced staff officers in the Joint United States Military Advisory Group (JUSMAG) in the Philippines was beneficial to both SOF and the embassy because they understood SOF missions and could assist in managing programs toward success for both security cooperation and SOF objectives.[15]

As for addressing the scope of the planning process to adequately account for a military-to-civilian handover of authority, one official with experience in Iraq underscored the need for SOF to invest in their

---

[11] Interview with U.S. military official, October 30, 2014.

[12] Interview with U.S. military official, October 30, 2014.

[13] Interview with U.S. military official, October 29, 2014.

[14] Interview with U.S. military official, October 29, 2014.

[15] Interviews with U.S. military officials, September–October 2014.

relationship with conventional forces and country teams. Particular attention must be paid to the fact that the embassy planning effort will have only a fraction of the military's personnel, and embassy personnel are unlikely to be familiar with the military's terminology.

Units complementary to SOF, such as civil-military support elements (CMSEs) and military information support teams (MISTs), provide the SOF enterprise with an opportunity to engender trust and goodwill within a country team in a manner that is unique to other military contributions. As seen in Jordan, when performing well these detachments can open doors for other SOF entities and mission sets.

In multiple embassies in Africa, including the case study of Uganda, a willingness to contribute to a small country team has engendered goodwill with SOF personnel. Though replicating aspects of this may be challenging in a larger embassy environment, there may be an opportunity to more generally incorporate SOF elements, or personnel familiar with SOF requirements, in some aspects of security cooperation efforts.

Challenge

Personnel limitations and space restrictions within the embassy can be put in place by the host nation, the State Department, or other entities. Many of these cannot be influenced by SOF but can hamper missions nevertheless.

Multiple officials commented on the difficulties associated with personnel number limits or space restrictions put in place by entities beyond SOF's control. In Pakistan, numbers of personnel were restricted due to limitations placed on the ODRP and the embassy by the Department of State. While the ambassador intervened on multiple occasions, it was often beyond the country team's ability to influence.[16] In the view of some, in Yemen there were issues that might have been avoided

---

[16] Interviews with U.S. military officials, September–October 2014.

had it not been for the six-thousand-mile screwdriver. There was some engineer study done on the Diplomatic Transit Facility–Sana'a (DTFS—the facility where U.S. personnel lived), and, just by looking at photos, someone in Diplomatic Security in Washington determined that the hotel wasn't safe in the wings, so everyone had to move to the core. Every senior leader was involved. It caused a lot of problems on the ground, even though no one from Washington ever came to actually look at the security situation. It was probably the most secure facility in all of Yemen.[17]

Another official who served in Yemen noted:

The ambassador made a request to increase personnel to carry out 1206 and 1208 programs, but these were vetoed by the Undersecretary of State for Management. General Mattis became actively engaged to try and get billets approved, but main State would not budge. This still hasn't been rectified. At one point, SOF had 115 folks in country, now it's down to fewer than 60.[18]

In Pakistan, the MIST initially had a basement office in the embassy, but later had to share it with the ODRP J1 (Personnel) office, in what was to be a temporary arrangement. When the ODRP took the office away, the MIST was forced to move to a single desk in the SOC Forward office and operate mainly out of a safehouse. Space limitations in the embassy compound often find Title 10 organizations at the bottom of the list for priority assignment.[19]

Implications for Afghanistan

The SOF element in U.S. Embassy Kabul should consider ways to incorporate building rapport and gaining trust with the country team, even if there is no immediate benefit. This will require an ongoing

---

[17] Interview with U.S. military official, October 7, 2014.

[18] Interview with U.S. military official, October 8, 2014.

[19] Interview with U.S. military official, October 7, 2014.

assessment of where the most useful bridges should be built (U.S. Agency for International Development, other government agencies, Public Diplomacy Office, etc.). Finding ways to assist other elements of the embassy in achieving their goals, sharing information and sources across the country team, and identifying candidates with the aptitude for working in an interagency environment can lead to mission success.

From the Iraq case study, one former U.S. Forces–Iraq official felt that bridging the cultural divide with State Department officials should begin with a frank dialogue early in the planning process. As they recommended, "Go to the embassy and ask, 'What do you need? What are you worried about, and what can SOF and the military do to help with your mission?' This opens a dialogue."[20] The interviewee went on to propose another practical way to establish relationships, "State guys and even conventional force guys love to be invited to the SOF compound to . . . have a meeting. Just that can be a significant gesture. It's a very small investment to build awareness and advocacy."[21]

To help address the embassy's capability gap when it comes to planning, an official with experience in Iraq recommended seconding relevant personnel to the embassy, not in a formal liaison role, but as full-time members of the country team. "I would go to the ambassador and say, 'I'll give you six planners.' . . . They are your people to do the work and serve as planners, interpreters, etc."[22] This was viewed as an important and useful element in understanding what it is the embassy wants to do and how the SOF element can help make it happen.

Besides planning, a general lack of experience and understanding when it came to the issue of authorities was cited in Iraq. One interviewee specifically noted that SOF authorities work differently from those of the conventional forces and that, if higher headquarters is not intimately aware of these distinctions, it can feed into broader communication issues. This interviewee went on to recommend that this should be an area of investment from the perspective of human

---

[20] Interview with U.S. military official, October 1, 2014.

[21] Interview with U.S. military official, October 1, 2014.

[22] Interview with U.S. military official, October 1, 2014.

resources and that "the best people on titles and authorities" should be sent to Afghanistan to take part in the planning process.[23]

The examples from Pakistan and Iraq demonstrate that the SOF element in Afghanistan can benefit from adopting a proactive approach to country team engagement and taking advantage of simple means of engendering goodwill. Incorporating relevant members of the country team in planning discussions and, to the extent possible, even allowing them to witness certain efforts firsthand can help to contest any biases and foster a shared sense of investment. Finally, it is important to get an early start in engaging with the country team for the transition to Chief of Mission authority. Doing so will both establish that the SOF element will be a conscientious, cooperative entity in the planning process and help to get all sides on the same page with regard to goals and objectives.

Finally, in Afghanistan, where space within the embassy complex is already at a premium, SOF leadership will have to deal with these issues on a case-by-case basis, but advance preparation and a basic understanding of which restrictions are firm and which are flexible can help SOF representatives navigate the complex bureaucracy of resource allocation in the embassy environment.

An anecdote from more recent months in Iraq illustrates how military personnel serving in an embassy ultimately serve at the discretion of the Chief of Mission. According to one interviewee, a MIST that has been serving in the embassy in Baghdad since the spring of 2014 may not be replaced when its deployment concludes in November 2014. Despite having built a good rapport with the Public Diplomacy and Political offices, the recently arrived ambassador believes in more traditional roles for embassy personnel and reportedly views the MIST as unnecessary. This should serve as less of a cautionary tale than as a reminder that, in some instances, the SOF element, through no fault of its own, could find its role limited by forces outside of its chain of command.

---

[23] Interview with U.S. military official, October 1, 2014.

CHAPTER THREE

Working with the Interagency: Stateside

The country team is guided and influenced by a number of strategic-level entities that have direct or indirect impact on the authorities, funding, and overall goals guiding the activities of the SOF enterprise and country team writ large. Decisions made at this level can affect interactions and relationships within the country team. It should be noted that, in this context, the interagency includes senior echelons of military leadership, such as the Pentagon and combatant commands.

Lessons Learned

In some cases, a lack of clear and compatible strategic guidance on goals and objectives from senior echelons in the United States to components in the field hampered planning and implementation at the country team level.

Due to factors that may be beyond the purview of the country team, strategic guidance outlining security assistance goals and objectives could be vague or otherwise incomplete during periods of transition. This can be expected to be an ongoing process that requires understanding the full range of U.S. interests in the country as well as demonstrating a high degree of flexibility, particularly in a rapidly evolving security and political environment. In Yemen, stalling and taking a competitive approach to tough decisions—in this case, the drawdown of U.S. personnel—served no one well, and ended with most of the SOC Forward going away. In Iraq, interviewees were unanimous in their opinion that guidance surrounding the post-2011 U.S. objectives and posture was in general vague and at times conflicting. The fact that the final decision that all troops were to be withdrawn by the end of the year was not conveyed until the September–October timeframe supports this. What resulted was a rushed and somewhat haphazard process of identifying which personnel would be prioritized for the limited Title 22 billets that would be available within the Office of Security Cooperation–Iraq.

Washington agencies, in particular the Pentagon and the State Department, as well as the combatant commands, play an influential role in establishing the authorities, privileges, and funding at the country level. This can have a significant impact on the status of interagency relationships within the country team, particularly when it comes to command and control and designated roles.

Regarding authorities and privileges, multiple officials felt that this is an often-overlooked aspect and that efforts should be made to identify and assign those with a detailed understanding of existing authorities for the various personnel and mission sets being discussed. Another aspect of this is having clearly delineated roles and chains of command for those operating in country prior to the transition. Ambiguity on this matter in Iraq made it more challenging for the military mission. According to one official, Office of Security Cooperation–Iraq and SOF interests were not represented at the senior-most levels of U.S. Central Command, as Iraq had to compete with other regional priorities, such as Iran and Syria, at a time when the State Department was prioritizing a more normalized relationship with Baghdad.[1] This reinforces the need for clear strategic guidance at the outset of the transition planning process, as well as the case for taking the initiative should guidance not be forthcoming.

According to senior military officials who worked in Pakistan, the most important keys to making the SOF/ODRP arrangement work were clear directives from the top-level of the Pentagon (both Gen.

---

[1] Interview with U.S. civilian official, October 27, 2014.

Dempsey's order and Special Operations Command Central directives; a good working relationship between the Chief of Mission, the
commander of U.S. military personnel, and senior officials from other
relevant government agencies; and strong personal relationships with
host-nation officials). When such relationships were frayed, operations
and cooperation suffered; when they were solid, cooperation flourished.

Clarifying directives that outline authorities and chains of command was essential to success in Pakistan and will likely be critical
to success in Afghanistan. In 2009, after the Chief of the ODRP was
made commander of all U.S. forces in Pakistan, there were some grow-
ing pains associated with bringing all SOF under his authority, but the
Special Operations Command Central commander "did a good job of
bringing SOF guys in line."[2] Eventually, the commander of U.S. forces
in Pakistan was able to report to the ambassador that "these guys work
for you" and was able to synergize missions across multiple lines of
authority and separate funding streams.[3]

Implications for Afghanistan

From a transitional standpoint, the transfer of authority in Iraq offers
the most salient comparison to Afghanistan. There, a lack of explicit
strategic guidance from the White House, coupled with a perceived
lack of ownership within the defense establishment, frustrated military leadership in Baghdad during the final months of the mission.
In the absence of clear guidance from Washington, SOF may need to
be proactive in clearly and carefully defining their mission in order to
get buy-in from the country team. A former U.S. Forces–Iraq official
endorsed such an approach should a similar issue arise in Afghanistan.
"I would advise SOF leadership that if they're not getting a clear signal,
write out SOF objectives for between 2014 and 2016 and then for post-
2016 and submit them for staffing through SOF and policymaking

---

[2] Interview with U.S. military official, September 18, 2014.

[3] Interview with U.S. military official, September 18, 2014.

entities."[4] This would act as a forcing function in a way that should not be viewed as overly critical or aggressive.

It is also important that the interagency make full use of the time it has to address issues regarding Afghanistan in the level of detail required. Unlike in Jordan, where a specific crisis resulted in a rapid influx of military and civilian personnel into the embassy, in Afghanistan the interagency planning process for the establishment of the SCO will be initiated well in advance. Thus, there should be sufficient time to work out the chain-of-command and authorities issues that were, in some instances, eschewed in Jordan prior to personnel deploying. Emphasizing this will be particularly important in Kabul, where the embassy will likely remain one of the United States' largest. The size of the embassy notwithstanding, one interviewee recommended that SOF leadership consider carefully the type and size of the element required in relation to its goals and objectives. Referring to Jordan, the official maintained that advocating for the highest possible headcount may not be most efficient, "A robust SOC Forward element was helpful, but extra people can create more work and new reliabilities on other personnel."[5]

---

[4] Interview with U.S. military official, October 1, 2014.

[5] Interview with U.S. military official, October 30, 2014.

CHAPTER FOUR

Working with the Host Nation

With the combat phase over, the coalitional aspect of the war is gradually giving way to what will be a series of bilateral relationships with the Afghan government. As part of the transition, SOF personnel will increasingly lose touch with operational- and tactical-level partner forces and thus depend on fewer strategic-level relationships for situational awareness. Additionally, changes in authorities and rules of engagement will necessitate adjustments on the part of both sides of the partnership. Maintaining the progress made thus far and continuing to develop Afghan capabilities will require U.S. leadership to work with Afghan counterparts in devising a way forward based on shared goals and expectations. Highlighting areas of prioritization and potential pitfalls will allow SOF leadership to address them early in the post-2016 planning process and avoid difficulties going forward.

Lessons Learned

A formal agreement in advance with the host/partner nation on interactions and expectations between U.S. missions and host/partner-nation missions goes a long way to avoiding misunderstandings, preventing operational difficulties, and enabling success.

U.S. SOF can be problematic for many host nations, because of perceived reputation or concerns about "the true nature" of SOF missions or because of mismatched national security interests of the

United States and the host nation. Such concerns can affect even the most innocuous training missions. SOF may also carry out priority U.S. missions that are of little interest to the host-nation government. The security assistance train and equip missions executed by the SCO for host-nation conventional military forces may be less objectionable to and a higher priority for the host nation, which may prefer that all U.S. funds and personnel be dedicated to that effort.

In Pakistan, for example, the Pakistani military wanted all U.S. funding to go toward its conventional forces rather than to the Frontier Corps fighting along the Afghan border. SOF was able to execute train and equip missions with the Frontier Corps in spite of Pakistani military resistance, until the bilateral relationship soured in 2011 in the wake of the Abbottabad raid that killed Osama bin Laden and the Raymond Davis Affair.[1] While the SOF training mission with the Frontier Corps was quickly cut and SOC Forward removed from country, Title 22 security assistance through the country team continued.

The signing of the Kapit Bisig agreement between the United States and the Philippines was more detailed than the typical security cooperation accord and outlined with great specificity the authorities and expected conduct of U.S. personnel operating in different parts of the country. This was credited as an overall benefit to the bilateral relationship, because it was negotiated ahead of time by both sides and left little open to interpretation by subordinate units.[2]

Building lasting bonds with host nation/partner-forces, especially those in higher ranks, can help to smooth fluctuations in the relationship between governments and increase the likelihood for obtaining necessary support.

Fostering relationships with host-nation officials at as high a level as possible is essential to mission success. As has sometimes been the case in Afghanistan, there was an uneasy relationship between the U.S. government and the Pakistani government, but several senior military

---

[1] Interview with U.S. military official, September 4, 2014.

[2] Interview with U.S. military official, September 2, 2014.

officers interviewed suggested that it was their "tight personal relationships" with key members of the host-nation military and intelligence leadership that enabled them to succeed.[3]

Several officials also suggested that positive relationships with Philippine officials enabled SOF to accomplish more, with fewer bureaucratic headaches than would have been the case in a nation with less shared history and fewer interpersonal connections. Where long-term relationships from a shared school experience in the United States were absent, as is the case in Afghanistan, both JUSMAG and SOF personnel sought to build longer-term bonds, either over the course of a two- to three-year tour in the case of the former, or over multiple repeat tours in the case of the latter. Most officers interviewed stressed the importance of building long-term relationships with host-nation forces, especially as the footprint decreases. This could either mean multiple tours interacting with host nation in the same period or longer tours in country.[4] A key component to building rapport with hostnation forces can be the personnel assigned to lead SOF efforts.

Challenge

Under the Leahy Act, SOF relationships with host-nation partners can become more problematic once SOF missions transition from Title 10 direct action or counterterrorism operations to Title 22 foreign assistance and security assistance.

In ongoing direct combat or counterterrorism operations, SOF will naturally partner with and seek assistance from individuals in the host-nation military or local area who have access to information, resources, authorities, and skills necessary to complete the mission. Concern is not usually given to the individual's personal history, but rather to what quid pro quo can be gained from an ongoing relationship. Security assistance, however, is limited by specific vetting require-

---

[3] Interviews with U.S. military officials, September 10–18, 2014.

[4] Interviews with U.S. military officials, September–October 2014.

ments under the Leahy Act that may hamper or end existing relationships as a transition occurs, or may otherwise affect SOF's ability to maintain rapport with certain individuals. One interviewee discussing Pakistan admitted that Leahy vetting can engender some wariness among local counterparts.[5]

Leahy vetting is a time-consuming and arduous process that requires close cooperation with the State Department and extremely careful relationship management with host-nation partners. It is not an insignificant event to have to tell the commander of host-nation forces that he may not attend a coveted conference or education opportunity in the United States because of concerns that he may, at some time in the past, have violated human rights protection provisions of the Leahy Act. Beyond concerns about Leahy, broader issues of funding and authorities for SOF partnerships may be tied directly to perceptions in Washington about SOF's host-nation partners and their past and ongoing actions.[6]

Implications for Afghanistan

SOF in Afghanistan should work through the country team to develop and gain approval for a memorandum of understanding or more formal agreement with the Afghan Ministry of Defense that outlines interactions and expectations between U.S. SOF missions and Afghan SOF missions. An agreement might cover rules of engagement, geographic areas of responsibility and/or sensitivity, supporting relationships, requirements and processes for mission clearance/approval/coordination, or guidelines for any other significant interaction or SOF mission that might provoke a negative reaction from host-nation military and civilian leadership. Though this may be an arduous pursuit, initiating discussions early in the planning process should make it feasible, and evidence suggests that such agreements pay dividends going forward.

---

[5] Interview with U.S. military official, September 4, 2014.

[6] Interview with U.S. civilian official, October 27, 2014.

Having been active in Afghanistan for more than a decade, U.S. SOF personnel have successfully developed solid relationships with a number of their Afghan counterparts. As transition looms, however, the SOF element should examine the extent to which changes in mission sets, authorities, funding, or any other factors may affect the nature of the interactions with Afghan security forces and their leadership.

Doing so proactively will allow SOF to communicate such changes to Afghan personnel and help to ensure that adjustments to overall U.S. policy will not negatively reflect on SOF.

Finally, prior to full transition to a limited SOF presence in a Title 22 role in the SCO, SOF leadership should map out future training and assistance plans and identify potential issues or problem areas associated with individuals or units whose history might invoke Leahy provisions or whose reputation in Washington might have a dampening effect on future programs. Early identification and adjudication of potential issues can help the SCO prevent fractured relationships in the future.

CHAPTER FIVE

Working within the SOF Community

In addition to identifying priorities for the SOF enterprise to consider as it prepares for transition in Afghanistan, this study illuminates ways in which SOF can best work with other relevant entities before and after the transition process. A handful of issues are unrelated to the interagency process, but could be addressed internally to the SOF community. Those issues follow.

Lessons Learned

Having program managers within the SCO who know and understand SOF requirements and programs improves SOF mission outcomes and enhances the SCO's mission. Too often, the SOF element placed as operational liaison to an embassy is unfamiliar with the functional procedures necessary to make security cooperation work.

Officials noted repeatedly that having a SOF-experienced officer in the SCO was an enormous benefit in translating SOF goals into potential SCO programs. The security force assistance and foreign internal defense missions of SOF can be similar to security assistance and security cooperation programs of the SCO, but are executed on different timelines, through different approval channels, and with different funding sources over a much different period of time. A former SCO official who had served in the Office of Defense Cooperation in Uganda explained, "A regular army security cooperation guy is more likely to want to remake the host-nation military in the U.S. image, whereas a SOF guy is more familiar with foreign internal defense, more used to working in diverse cultural environments."[1]

Another official suggested, however, that from a programmatic standpoint the SOF enterprise could do more to contribute to the day-to-day function of the SCO:

> The guy working in a SCO doesn't have to be an 18, but he has to understand SOF and the program management aspects of SCO duties.[2] SOF leadership needs to ensure that there are personnel with SOF experience and knowledge in the SCO.

Others noted that some liaison officers assigned by SOF in the embassy were too junior, too unfamiliar with embassy procedures and culture, or too incapable of integrating well into the relationshiporiented embassy environment. One SOF commander in Yemen left relationship building and liaison with embassy staff to his sergeant major. He said:

> The sergeant major took all the ankle-biter stuff and made the embassy more amenable to SOF staff. He understood you had to play ball with the embassy, even down to the more minute details, such as hosting social events. In an embassy, you have to be out there a lot. State Department people are more social. We made a lot of money hosting events for people in the embassy.[3]

Echoing a sentiment that several interviewees voiced, one who served in the Philippines stated, "The best liaison officers could take off their uniform, put on a coat and tie, and mingle with the embassy staff."[4]

---

[1] Interview with U.S. military official, August 28, 2014.

[2] 18 is the military occupational specialty code for a special operations officer in the U.S. Army.

[3] Interview with U.S. military official, October 7, 2014.

[4] Interviews with U.S. military officials, September–October 2014.

SOF missions led by a diplomatic and persuasive commander who coordinates closely with the country team will more likely enjoy interagency support, even when circumstances turn challenging. In the case of partners in Yemen, proximity and close coordination helped SOF and the country team understand each other's priorities and identify areas for cooperation. In contrast, the SOC Forward was less integrated with the country team, and any missteps in its work with host-nation officials that were brought to the country team's attention could more easily lead to lingering frustration rather than quick resolution.

Some level of specialized predeployment training for SOF personnel assigned to an embassy, akin to that undertaken by other military personnel assigned to a SCO, should be provided. This will help SOF personnel to manage their own expectations and work within the management timelines and decision cycles of other embassy offices.

SOF tend to work at a faster pace than most other organizations on the country team, gathering information, making decisions, and taking actions, often with deadly effect, in a very short decision cycle.[5] This is partly a function of differences in organizational culture, but it is also due to differences in mission timelines and tour lengths. Embassy personnel will be executing Title 22 program budgets that were put in place by their predecessors three years earlier, and they will be executing whole-of-government strategies and theater security cooperation plans that have long planning lead times and longer horizons for mission accomplishment.

SOF will be executing the commander's intent with daily and weekly mission accomplishment and updates. SOF will be used to working 24/7 for a shorter tour, whereas the embassy staff will be working 8 a.m. to 5 p.m., five to seven days a week, on a two-year, three-year, or longer tour and are more likely to be closely attuned to the host nation's normal work tempo and decision cycles.[6]

---

[5] Interview with U.S. military official, October 8, 2014.

[6] Interview with U.S. military official, September 28, 2014.

As one official noted, "We are victims of our own systems. We are information junkies. We need information continuously, but in an embassy you often find yourself outrunning the decisionmaking of the country team."[7]

While the size of the SOF liaison element and rank(s) of its personnel can vary greatly depending on the SOF footprint and mission set, on multiple occasions interviewees noted that SOF personnel rarely received specialized training prior to serving in an embassy and, in some instances, have competing responsibilities unrelated to the liaison aspect. In some cases, a liaison is a member of an Operational Detachment–Alpha (a small team of SOF personnel) and is simply told to serve in the embassy just prior to arriving in country. This makes SOF personnel vulnerable to avoidable missteps and not having a clear understanding of the operational environment in which they will be serving.

SOF operating under Title 10 will be able to operate with greater freedom of movement and with fewer bureaucratic hurdles than SCO and SOF personnel operating under Title 22. Title 10 SOF, however, may find it harder to access embassy facilities, funding, and logistical support managed by the embassy.

Where Title 10 forces are not directly under Chief of Mission authorities, they will be able to make their own risk assessments concerning force protection and move about the country under their own supervision. Likewise, they can manage their own safehouses and logistics, will be free from concerns about Leahy vetting, and can interact directly with the host nation in their areas of responsibility. Once under Chief of Mission authority in the embassy, however, a number of restrictions and coordination wickets will encumber their activities. Embassy regional security officers (RSOs), responsible for the safety and security of embassy personnel in country tend to be more risk averse than their U.S. Department of Defense counterparts, especially in today's post-Benghazi environment. But working out of the

---

[7] Interview with U.S. military official, October 8, 2014.

embassy under Title 10 authorities comes with its own set of restrictions. According to one senior official interviewed:

> In Pakistan, State [Department] was uneasy about the status of the Title 10 forces, and who had responsibility for their day-today tasks. There was a lot of pushback within State about Title 10 staff getting housing, funding, RSO authorization, etc. The facilities staff saw them as not really part of the embassy staff.[8]

A close working relationship with the ambassador can ameliorate these concerns. As one official in Pakistan noted, "the ambassador was very effective at blowing away bureaucratic obstacles."[9]

Challenge

The recent cap on SOF deployments to six months makes it difficult to build and maintain relationships within an embassy and has raised concern among numerous ambassadors. Interviewees provided no solutions to this challenge, as it is internally created, but many recommended extending the tour length or seeking repetitive assignments to the same embassy.

Numerous interviewees cited one significant limiting factor in realizing their potential vis-à-vis the country team: limits on duration of tours. While such a cap was seen as an understandable necessity in an era of persistent overseas operations, there was a consensus among respondents that USSOCOM should consider granting an exception for units that do not endure the same kinetic operational tempo as direct-action elements.

In an embassy environment, such brief tours can prevent CMSEs and MISTs, for example, from obtaining the deeper, contextual understanding of both local atmospherics and the broader embassy agenda. Short tour lengths were described as problematic by multiple officials

---

[8] Interview with U.S. military official, September 10, 2014.

[9] Interview with U.S. military official, September 10, 2014.

with experience working in an embassy environment, where a typical tour lasts two or three years. In Jordan, for example, largely because of short tour lengths and the time required to come up to speed on the embassy's strategic communications plan and host-nation dynamics, the ambassador viewed the MIST as more of a burden than an asset and eventually sent the entire unit home.[10]

Similarly, in Iraq, the U.S. ambassador reportedly does not like short tour lengths. He is concerned that SOF feel that they can come in to country, do some haphazard things, and then be replaced. He asked USSOCOM for a waiver on the tour length, but it was denied.[11]

In the Philippines, the Air Force liaison coordination element rotated in and out of country on a 90-day basis. This relatively short period spent in country diminished their effectiveness, and this was mitigated only by the fact that a large percentage of the team had previously rotated to the mission.[12]

Implications for Afghanistan

For SOF missions within the SCO in Afghanistan to be successful, planners should seek to establish billets within the SCO that will be coded for SOF experienced career fields. Officers and senior noncommissioned officers (NCOs) in the SCO who know and understand SOF requirements and programs will enhance the potential for successful SOF and SCO mission outcomes. One interviewee suggested that SOF leadership should interact with the SCO planning team in Afghanistan and get involved in writing the requirements for the necessary manning/billets.[13] This will ensure the appropriate experience and knowledge are represented among the SCO staff.

The force provider(s) for SOF billets in the SCO must prepare SOF personnel before they transition into an embassy environment and

---

[10] Interview with U.S. military official, October 30, 2014.

[11] Interview with U.S. military official, October 1, 2014.

[12] Interview with U.S. military official, September 3, 2014.

[13] Interview with U.S. civilian official, September 3, 2014.

assist them in expectation management once they have been assigned. Understanding and working within the informational and decision cycles of other embassy offices will minimize friction. Navigating the bureaucracy and administration of various streams of funding is not easy. SOF officers who might have to be responsible for administration of Title 22 funds or who may be embedded within the SCO should receive the benefit of training at the Defense Institute of Security Assistance Management.

While the details of the transition and eventual footprint of SOF forces in Afghanistan post-2016 remain undecided, it is safe to say that a significant share of SOF personnel remaining in country will operate under Title 22 authorities. This will affect, perhaps dramatically, the degree of independence that SOF will be able to exercise regarding freedom of movement, logistics, housing, and a host of other areas that must be considered during planning phases. Should a Title 10 presence endure, SOF leadership should weigh carefully how to best assign its personnel—in an environment where the Chief of Mission has primacy, there are benefits and drawbacks to each designation.

Optimally, the deployment tour length for SOF serving in U.S. Embassy Kabul would be one or two years, in alignment with other agencies and positions. Barring that change to policy, SOF should seek to rotate individuals repeatedly through the same positions in the SCO, so that relationships and familiarity with the mission and environment can be built over subsequent tours.

Final Consideration: Might a Special Operations Liaison Officer Be Suitable for Kabul at Some Point?

Jordan demonstrates that, in a nation where SOF has a robust footprint and a diverse mission set, the appointment of a special operations liaison officer (SOLO) can bring both improved synchronization and a degree of institutional knowledge appreciated by the rest of the country team. Depending on the eventual layout of the SCO in Kabul, it may be worth considering a permanent SOLO and staff under Title 22 authorities there. Even if the construct is initially deemed impractical to manage given the size and scope of the post-2016 mission, it could become more appropriate in the later years as the footprint declines. A SOLO-led team falling under Title 22 authority would be under at least one-year orders, with preference for two-year orders or longer, according to a subject-matter expert.[14] Family support may not be available in Kabul, so these lengthier assignments may be less attractive to SOF officers, or they may be deemed unsupportable. However, the lesson of the Jordan experience is that the longer and more formal the assignment, the more likely the SOLO and other SOF personnel are to build successful and lasting relationships within the embassy.

Implications for Afghanistan

Though determining the practicality of appointing a SOLO in Kabul is beyond the scope of this study, the potential utility such an assignment there was cited by some officials. One interviewee suggested a way to improve upon the Jordan model to make a similar construct in Kabul more feasible. The SOF liaison element, headed by a SOLO, could be designed to mirror SOF functions. A five-person team might be more effective than the three-person team currently stationed in Amman. These five positions would be[15]

1. SOLO
2. administrative NCO
3. senior NCO
4. intelligence NCO or officer
5. public affairs, civil affairs, or military information support operations NCO or officer.

This last position—number 5—could be expanded to three separate positions to facilitate all potential SOF activities supported by USSOCOM and U.S. Central Command. In this case, the liaison ele-

---

[14] Interview with U.S. military official, September 23, 2014.

[15] Interview with U.S. military official, September 23, 2014.

ment would consist of at least seven SOF personnel. Command relationships between the SOLO and SOF elements in the country may or may not exist in Afghanistan. In Jordan, the relationships are flexible, depending on the mission and element assigned. One interviewee suggested that the commander should be located where he can be most effective; either within the embassy or in the field.[16]

The other case study that provoked the mention of SOLOs was Uganda, which is relevant to Afghanistan insofar as a regional SOF effort is under deliberation. Tying in this consideration with the issue of having two SOC Forwards operating in that country, Special Operations Command Africa (SOCAFRICA) has reportedly considered combining the two elements into one command that would permit a more streamlined interface with the rest of the country team. Discussions, however, have been stymied by SOCAFRICA's preference to remain oriented around specific threats, in this case the mission to counter the Lord's Resistance Army and the African Union Mission in Somalia (AMISOM), instead of regions.[17] A possible way to ameliorate this would be to assign a permanent SOLO to the embassy in Kampala to serve as a single point of synchronization and interface with the country team. According to an official, however, while Uganda is one of the top priorities for the establishment of a SOLO billet, this is reportedly caught up in disputes regarding National Security Decision Directive 38 for the time being.[18]

---

[16] Interview with U.S. military official, September 23, 2014.

[17] Interview with U.S. military official, October 1, 2014.

[18] National Security Decision Directive 38, *Staffing at Diplomatic Missions and Their Overseas Constituent Posts*, Washington, D.C.: The White House, June 2, 1982; interview with U.S. military official, October 1, 2014